THE HOPEFUL HAT

Carole Satyamurti (1939-2019) was a poet and sociologist. For many years she taught at the Tavistock Clinic, where her main academic interest was in the relevance of psychoanalytic ideas to an understanding of the stories people tell about themselves, whether in formal autobiography or in social encounters. She co-edited *Acquainted with the Night: psychoanalysis and the poetic imagination* (Karnac, 2003). She won the National Poetry Competition in 1986, and a Cholmondeley Award in 2000. Her *Selected Poems* (Oxford University Press, 1998) was reissued by Bloodaxe Books in 2000. Her *Mahabharata: A Modern Retelling* (W.W. Norton, 2015) was joint winner of the inaugural Roehampton Poetry Prize.

Her Bloodaxe retrospective, *Stitching the Dark: New & Selected Poems* (2005), drew on five collections: *Broken Moon* (1987), *Changing the Subject* (1990), *Striking Distance* (1994), *Love and Variations* (2000), and *Stitching the Dark* (2005). Two of these were Poetry Book Society Recommendations. This was followed by two later collections, *Countdown* (2011), and her final collection, *The Hopeful Hat*, also a Poetry Book Society Recommendation, published posthumously in 2023.

CAROLE SATYAMURTI

The Hopeful Hat

BLOODAXE BOOKS

Copyright © Emma Satyamurti 2023

ISBN: 978 1 78037 653 0

First published 2023 by
Bloodaxe Books Ltd,
Eastburn,
South Park,
Hexham,
Northumberland NE46 1BS.

www.bloodaxebooks.com
For further information about Bloodaxe titles
please visit our website and join our mailing list
or write to the above address for a catalogue.

Supported using public funding by
**ARTS COUNCIL
ENGLAND**

Cover design: Gregory Warren Wilson, Neil Astley & Pamela Robertson-Pearce

Digital reprint of the 2023 Bloodaxe Books edition

CONTENTS

IV

FOREWORD

My mother, Carole Satyamurti, died in University College Hospital, London on 13th August 2019, sooner than expected after receiving a diagnosis of terminal cancer. Many conversations were left un-had, including about the poems contained in this collection. She had been working on it for some time but had not yet submitted it to her publisher or given any other definitive indication that she considered the work finished. Our greatest clue as to her intentions was that the poems were printed out and organised in a way that suggested the shape she envisaged for the book, but with notes making clear that a few of the individual poems were to some extent still work in progress.

The biggest project of Satyamurti's* later years was her book *Mahabharata: A Modern Retelling* (W.W. Norton, 2015) in which she rendered the vast and vivid Indian epic in 800 pages of what Philip Pullman describes as 'supple and muscular verse'. The book took some eight years to complete, taking Satyamurti into new and consuming creative territory. After it was finished, I think she felt in some way disconnected from the voice that had breathed the life and meaning into her earlier lyric poems. The poems here mark her re-finding of that voice, familiar from *Countdown* (Bloodaxe Books, 2011), the last collection published during her lifetime, and from earlier work.

The question of what a voice can represent is a thread running though Satyamurti's work, often interrogated in particular in relation to poetry itself – how and to what extent poems, and words more broadly, count in the face of suffering and injustice. We see that exploration continued here, for example in the title-poem, and in 'Small Change', 'Paper Boat', and 'Hold On' which ends:

---

* After a good deal of thought as to how best to refer to my mother in this context and with every option seeming not quite right, I have followed convention in using her surname only. E.S.

7

Don't be afraid to make a poem
raw as sandpaper. And even though
a million protests, twice as many feet,
couldn't stop a war, get out there
with your small voice, your light tread.

By the time of writing the poems in this collection, Satyamurti's
interest in the impact and importance of voice and words had
been overlaid by a cruel irony. A diagnosis of laryngeal cancer
in 2012 had led to the removal of her voice-box and part of her
tongue, a loss she bore with courage and resilience. She charts
this experience and its consequences in the sequence of poems
that starts with 'Voicing the Void'. In 'Sea Change' she writes:

I mouth words as if you were a foreigner,
ration them to crude essentials.
How redundant most words are.

Yet while her voicelessness may have sharpened her awareness
of the verbiage common in everyday conversation, the power
of words well-used is simultaneously highlighted. It is of course
no accident that our word 'language' derives from the Latin
word for tongue. Nowhere more strikingly than in 'Glossal'
does Satyamurti distil the essential relationship between being
human and the ability to speak (out):

What prudent torture it was,
to cut out dissident tongues,
knowing that the subtlest manoeuvres

of this most potent sixty grams of flesh –
this truth-teller, this incendiary organ,
this evolutionary achievement
as vital to the human core of us
as the heart is – can shift the world.

The posthumous publication of these late poems adds a yet
deeper layer to the question of Satyamurti's voice; what space
might it now occupy, how might it live on? As her daughter I

cannot come to this objectively – her voice is the first sound I remember, with its cadences of invitation and consolation; it is the other, wiser, half of conversations to keep for life; the descant line of songs belted out in harmony; in its internalised form it can persecute in that special way unique to mothers; and in unguarded moments it is the ringing silence of her absence.

But of course her voice – though now entirely disembodied – is still here, speaking to us through the poems with an often uncanny relevance as she wrestles with how to think about and make sense of impermanence and death. 'You Could Say', 'Shore-line', 'Memento Mori' and '*Le moment juste*' are just some examples.

This theme of 'stitching the dark' runs through Satyamurti's previous work too, but this time is different; the dark is no longer only figurative. For me it has been both unnerving and heartening to discover, after she died, poems which articulate, and also seem to respond to, my own more prosaic struggle to understand what her death means. 'Inheritance', for instance, answered with supernatural specificity that watershed question of what to keep and what to let go.

While these final poems will inevitably hold particular reson- ances for those who knew Satyamurti personally, they are about the challenge of facing our mortality, of finding meaning despite (and because of) it; an endeavour which is as quintessentially human as language.

In 'Solid', the last poem of this last collection, after describing the permanent nature of atoms Satyamurti leaves us with this characteristically clear-eyed question:

> But there's no denying
> one day you will be dead
> and where do the colours go
> when the carpet fades?

EMMA SATYAMURTI
London, 2022

ACKNOWLEDGEMENTS

'Memento Mori' was written in response to 'Festoni: Natura Morta', a series of paintings by Helen Wilks shown at Studio Ex Purgamento, London, in 2016. An earlier version of this poem was published in the gallery's catalogue for that exhibition. To our knowledge, no other poem has been printed or published anywhere prior to its appearance in this book.

We wish to thank Carole Satyamurti's literary executor, Gregory Warren Wilson, for his meticulous work in preparing the manuscript of *The Hopeful Hat* for publication.

I

The Hopeful Hat

At the bus stop, a dishevelled woman
in drab clothing much too big for her,
is blowing a bright pink descant recorder.
Beside her, on the ground, a hopeful hat.

Staring straight ahead, she blows 'toot toot',
child-like, flat, a mournful open note
over and over, the sound short as her breath.
I pass her several times across the morning.

The smug Victorian clock tower marks the quarters.
Still she blows 'toot toot', the dreary, stubborn
single note, dying as her breath fails.
The hat holds few coins. I think to speak to her,

ask how it has come to this, standing here
beside her hopeful hat; and could she not
manage at least one tune, like the gypsy
near Tesco – even if the rhythm's wrong?

I don't of course, restrained by that endemic
English malady, embarrassment.
Her one hopeless note follows me home,
and here I write my shabby conscience out.

Cans

After the first can he was sad as ever.

After the second he was quarrelsome.

After the third he began to smile

and then... and then...

to sing
to forgive his brother
to dance (a bit floppily)
to preach in tongues
to solve the problems of the Middle East

after which
he left his body.

There should be a heavenly homecoming
for one who had no future except this.

How to Wash Dishes on the Eightfold Path

Stack the plates, the graceful spoons,
each perfect for its purpose. Notice
the music of clatter and jingle
never quite like this before, ever.

Relish gleaming surfaces
rescued from smears and encrustation;
the alchemy of matter out of place
as food becomes rubbish.

You are enacting the changefulness
of all things, the swing between order
and chaos. A broken bowl becoming
a charged fragment in your hand

invites you to consider now, and now,
the quiddity of all that is.

You Could Say

it all comes down to fate,
fortune's fork flipping us this way or that,
though there's choice in not choosing;
we have responsibilities.

Partially sighted, we peer
over time's precipice
which, soon or later,
we'll topple from.

For now,
other people's smoke
rises from the chimney
dispersing into thick air.

Obituary

Over the page
your name leaps at me
my first love
the photograph, recent, effaces
my memory of you.
You still had your thick hair though.

Last month, daughter in mind,
I put in the recycling
all our letters from fifty years ago,
and remembered how painful it was then,
how guarded I was,
– flown back from Africa
to lie with you in my rented basement room,
before your drive back to your needy wife.
How I ached for you.

That was always the deal. It was always
the sex, though I loved your brilliance.
'In love' is an ordinary illness,
an insanity. Politically we were far apart.
It was never going further.
After your new marriage
friendly for a while. Then silence.

Not grief, after so long, but curiosity –
what happens to such vivid passion;
does it inhabit some enduring niche,
conditioning other loves?
What's to be done with random memories:
your slight Black Country twang,
your distinctive fingernails. Your teasing.
Me humming Gounod to your Bach.
Penshurst in the rain: fiasco.

What does one do with past selves –
lock them in; embroider them; forget them;
draw lessons? Or acknowledge them,
like books that formed one once
but won't be read again?

Among the letters
was a manuscript – a poem
by Baudelaire you had set for me.
Held back from recycling, I had decided
to send it on your birthday
with, perhaps, a short message.
Out of the blue.

Wednesday is collection day.

Inheritance

I woke up worrying –
how would all my possessions
fit into my daughter's small house?

It was as if I couldn't let go
as if the possessions were my life
and she should preserve it
after I'm dead.

All my things – what a waste
if they should be scattered unloved,
stripped of their patina
of meanings and memories.

The thought was an attempt to stay death –
as if I wouldn't be truly dead
if the objects in my life could be
re-configured in my daughter's –
my life grafted seamlessly onto hers.

I walked from room to room
and realised there was almost nothing
she would want – the Indian bronzes maybe,
the Zanzibar chest,
the cupboard with the painted birds?

How could I have thought there would be
a problem? Had I imagined
that my whole life's experience
would be assimilated into, crammed
into hers, and she too small to carry it?

Wednesday Again

The clatter of bin men
blocking the roadway:
collection day again.
Surely it can't be a week
since last Wednesday.
Is it repeating itself? Am I?

Collections are becoming
more frequent. Soon
it will be Wednesday
twice a week. I won't be able
to feed the recycling bin
fast enough. So…

I'll have to draw on reserves –
unread books, drawers stuffed
with past tax returns, love letters,
diaries, outdated lecture notes.
And what metal can I find?
What glass? What old boxes?

I know – in the end
Wednesdays will be arriving
ever faster, bonnet to bumper
until they overtake me,
revving, speeding onward,
leaving me behind for good.

New York

I come alive here. Not seeing the supposed unfriendliness
the rush and drivenness. The Hudson seems to give the city
breath, make it spacious. Just to walk the streets gives glimpses
of a million secrets, while I remain invisible. If I stood still,
perhaps I would draw the odd shyster, eye to the main chance,
so I impersonate a native, as if I knew what the next block
will deliver, learning how to stare without staring.

The enchantment, the romance of it. As if poets, playwrights
might pass me any minute, inhabiting their legendary names.
This precise mixture of strange and familiar is how I'd live
always, if I could start over in another life. Sometimes
it's unbearable that there is only one for each of us
and that the carpet rolls up so very briskly behind us.
But being a stranger is by its nature an impermanence.

Easter

Have you been in at the birth
of green groping from black;
seen new leaves hanging slack
wrung out by effort, earth

hazy with the thrust
of countless urgent tips
out of innumerable sleeps;
and wondered at this lust

for resurrection? Is it the stuff
of blind habit? Or a benighted
sense that, though it's blighted,
the world's still good enough?

All that Is Solid Melts into Air

(Karl Marx)

It's about state of the art, cutting edge,
the flash cash appeal of high-rise,
gleaming screens and open-plan,
hot desking, watching your back.

It's being quick off the block
shaving a bit off on the side
like everyone, and your tongue
gets fat with blagging.

So you've got to have a laugh
on a Friday, a few drinks,
a line or two, chat up the girls
to remind yourself who you are.

II

Voicing the Void

1

I will never mistake myself
for a decibel
now I can no longer
sing
whistle
play the recorder
shout to save my life.

2

'One of these days,' said my friend, Raju,
'there'll be an instrument so fine,
so tuned to the subtlest vibrations
pulsing still in the air around us,
that we'll recover the voice of Lord Krishna
exhorting Arjuna to take up arms
on the battlefield of Kurukshetra.' *

He was serious. I thought – how could he,
a man schooled in respect for evidence,
take an ancient text so literally,
be innocent of how a poem can fly
free of facts to furnish the mind's ear
with wonders sprung from imagining?

But now my voice-box has been cut away
I remember Doctor Raju – his conviction,
his devoutly wished for instrument;
imagine my life's piled up utterance
cluttering the ether like space junk,
part of humanity's monstrous din
drowning out the wisdom of the gods.

---

* This refers to an episode in the *Bhagavad Gita*.

New Year on T14

On *Head and Neck*, we're at the window
with our drip-stands and drainage bottles,
fourteen floors nearer infinity.
Continuous tail-lights on the Euston Road
are rubies strung across wet tarmac.

It's quiet up here. I think of peacocks
some people keep for their gorgeousness
and have the screech surgically removed.
Not that any of us looks remotely gorgeous
in our assorted, graceless dressing gowns.

To the south – Parliament, the London Eye.
Now it's midnight, and the rain's not quenching
rockets soaring mute above the river.
There must be bangs and whistles, but from here
it's all spectacle – flashing stars, bright parabolas,

zigzags we can imagine transforming water
to shimmering silk. We have a royal view
and applaud, smiling at one another, loving
how vivid they are, those glorious explosions;
sorry at how soon the show is over.

Glossal

Tongue is truncated, thickened.
It's forked, like a serpent's,
but it can still move, still articulate,
still, with difficulty, shift a gobbet
from one cheek to the other.

A drunkard or a prisoner would be glad
to utter words as compromised as these.
What prudent torture it was,
to cut out dissident tongues,
knowing that the subtlest manoeuvres

of this most potent sixty grams of flesh –
this truth-teller, this incendiary organ,
this evolutionary achievement
as vital to the human core of us
as the heart is – can shift the world.

Sea Change

1

With a hole where voice used to be
there's no more singing, calling,
blowing candles out. No natural speech.

I mouth words as if you were a foreigner,
ration them to crude essentials.
How redundant most words are.

Prosthetic voice is the sound of daleks,
rusty locks and serious bronchitics.
No choice of register, no expressiveness.

I'm not complaining. As the saying goes,
'Worse things happen at sea.'
Speaking of which...

2

... if I drew up a list of losses
I'd add the sea.
I was amphibian once,
the sea my other natural element,
shouting as waves curled above me,
diving through, not knowing
when I'd breathe again.

Now, my neck pierced like an organ pipe,
the sea would pour in as an anthem
from the beginning of the world –
a roar, reclaiming me.

Necklace of Wasps

Not long since ordinary days
when neck was just neck
and chin was becoming double.

Now chin juts from its stalk
as if asserting something
like survival. Like keeping on.

'Like a necklace of wasps,'
I tell the doctor. It's obvious
she doesn't know what I mean.

Sometimes I feel their soft feet
brushing my clavicle. Exploring
the limits of their territory.

More often, they sting,
malicious. Plenty more venom
where that comes from.

Voice is capricious,
strangled, or a repertoire
of frog-like utterance

but wasps won't eat my words,
even if I must chop up my sentences
to spit them out.

Let this be my last word on the subject.
The wasps sting and stab
but, ignoring them, I speak.

Mother Tongue

One hundred years ago today
my mother arrived, spoiled youngest,
inheriting grandmother's timid genes
and the beauty that would be a drawback.

'Talkative and vain' – the verdict
of the school report she laughed about.
'Old frumps, they were just jealous.'
In another life, she might have been a star.

At ninety-seven she finally gave up
the daily argument with the mirror:
gnarled fingers gripping lipstick, tracing
shrunken outlines she could no longer see.

Who was she when speech gave up on her?
Was she a star when, lacking words of her own,
she would 'Singalongamax', word-perfect,
Mr Sandman... Show me the way to go home.

Overtones

Without voice of my own,
other people's voices come alive,
saying things they don't intend
like harmonics accidentally plucked.

Those un-owned emotions weigh on me.

Beyond their mundane utterance,
I hear their grief, anxiety, the way
they criticise companions, silently.
When I respond, they are amazed
as though I had touched their most intimate parts.

III

Requiem for a Death Foretold

It sheltered all of us, that was the point,
  stable
so that inside, if nowhere else, we were
    the just about managing
all equal – as we will be at life's end.
    strong
Our building was the envy of the world.
  responsibility
Then we let chancers bring their bank accounts,
  deliver
grab choice pieces for themselves, so that
    promise
through cracks, hairline at first, unnoticed,
  fairness
air-borne moisture seeped into the walls.
    secure
Iron streaks appeared, blood-coloured oxides
    certainty
wept, widening the fissures; degraded steel
  trust
split what had seemed so solid.
    for everyone
Crumbling pillars, spilling flakes of rust,
  control
collapsed at last.
    not just the few
Where to turn? Now where can we find
  our society
a haven from inevitable shocks?
  we will
'Trust us,' say the fat chancers,
    no magic money tree
'our palace will protect you.' At a cost.

Small Change

This must be the room of last resort,
this half-lit passage under the dripping bridge
where, on the only route to the Underground,
you pass four, sometimes more, rough sleepers
strung out at intervals against the wall,

the same, day after day, week after week.
Some are mounds under filthy quilts,
some sit, savaged by the wind, as if
stunned by trains thundering overhead.
Even when it's quiet, they don't call out,

but sit behind their empty paper cups,
faces drained ash pale, or red-complexioned
with that alcoholic, weather-roughened look.
I want them gone. I want to be absolved.
Shall I give some coins to each of them?

If it were only one... Or just one day...
In the chasm between me and them hangs
dis-ease. Step after step, I stare ahead,
fixed on my warm and well-shaped destination.
What has a poem got to do with this?

Paper Boat

I used to
when it was
just a craft
not a reminder
not mockery of
desperate traffic
flimsy dinghies
lives drowned
by the holdful.

Fingers clumsy
I could take
this newspaper
the world's griefs
in its folds, revive
the knack, make
another vessel
sodden words
sinking.

Vyasa's Gift*

A single life has so many
seemingly irreparable harms.
But, that one night, there would be
miraculous amends.

The moon rose above the lake, and
slowly rising dripping from the water –
old friends to whom, distracted,
we had given too little love.

Enemies too – except that, now,
everything was understood
and the word seemed silly –
as in some childish game of soldiers.

How we thirsted for it not to end
but then, once we gave up on clinging,
relinquishing regret was possible.
Love tasted new, unsullied.

The vision faded. Afterwards,
when the lake was mirror-still again,
all seemed unchanged.
Nothing would ever be the same.

---

* This refers to an episode in the Indian epic, *Mahabharata*.

Hold On

Hold on to the real news,
to what you know is of good report.
Hold on to what you know of fakery
nail a lie when you hear one,
spot bluster on the public highway.

Fine-tune your ear to subtext,
manipulation and duplicity.
Ask yourself who benefits,
whose hopes are cruelly raised,
who dares get away with what.

Don't be afraid to make a poem
raw as sandpaper. And even though
a million protests, twice as many feet,
couldn't stop a war, get out there
with your small voice, your light tread.

The Climate Game

Start on safe ground with ICE words
glaze   creak   glisten
    crack   craze   shimmer
sparkle   tinkle   crunch   dazzle
    glacier   frost   soften
        shrink   melting into

WATER

        gush   drip
meander   trickle   bubble
        gurgle   flow   cascade
    lap   flood   drown   monsoon
    gulp   condense
            becoming what we call

AIR

oxygen   steam   ozone
            vapour   fog
tornado   breath
        haar   gas   sirocco
            all varieties of cloud

Weigh each word
as though it were the last word in the world;
let it go.
        No one wins.
It is not that kind of game.

War Rhyme

The leaves are turning,
time is rewound.
For the beautiful boy
dead on the sand
there is no more time,
no returning.
Was it an accident?
Was it a crime?

Flotsam... jetsam...
who is to blame?
A year or two on
we've forgotten his name
and how he drowned
with his mother and brother;
and the forces that killed him
remain the same.

He could have been mine,
he could have been yours.
It's our politicians
who bar the doors;
our neighbours who say
the country's full,
who want more security,
fences. A wall.

Grand

If you strike the keys
they whine like shells,
like the taste of sour milk.
Notes ricochet and die.

The piano stands alone. Wind
whistles in through shattered panes
rubble crunches under foot.
A familiar story. But today

a restorer has flown in from Paris.
She has brought stringing hooks,
tuning pin reamer, damper heads,
action leather, glues and polishes...

hope's stubborn paraphernalia.
Don't say, 'What's the point?'
Don't say, 'This is an empty metaphor.'
It is a piano. It is recovering its voice

and even if it will be smashed again,
first it will deliver clear, true notes;
and a girl will sit down to play
a piece she knows by heart.

IV

Debrief

Of the first thirty astronauts, only seven marriages survived.

Guardian, 4 October 2017

Through the window
the turning world was a bauble
glowing blue on infinite black;
drifts of cloud like tulle wrapping
draped around its shoulders.

'What was it like?' – over and over
on the street, on air, on line, until
words lose their meaning. They want
a piece of you as though you were
moon rock; comfort food.

Maybe it's like the trenches – knowledge
of what humankind is capable of trashing
hideous beyond words. Our cosmically
insignificant habitat, riven by hurricanes,
parched and flooded: all we have.

You draw up to your once-familiar door.
Who knew love could be so friable?
Hearing loss. You see her speak as if
through glass, part of you still out there;
the part that will never be at home.

Ought

I should be at the gym
slogging on the treadmill
fending off crippledom –

though I've no incentive. I fear
a few machines won't defend me
from wasting and wear and tear.

How feeble it makes me feel
that, instead, I'm vegetating
in a chair with paper and pencil

yanking at arbitrary rhymes
for a poem that won't work,
since mere chimes

do not a poem make.
Maybe I'll do a few step-ups
on the stairs – or take

a brisk walk up the hill –
though might I not do just as well
with a multivitamin pill?

Sight Reading

It's coordination – that's the problem.
Cello... recorder... even singing
I can more or less keep going
but two staves reduce my hands
to palsy, eyes to jitter bugs.

Perhaps there's some deep refusal
of harmonious twoness – as when
I asked you to move out, and the house
returned to sounding its single note
then settled back to silence.

Succulent

1

Freezing on the side-line, told to cheer,
I'm watching the home game,
the smarter-kitted visitors from Kinnaird Park
bigger, with more fleshy knees.
It seems our side is winning

– though I'm vague about the rules.
All winter, by a mix of guile, manipulation
and hiding in the classroom cupboard
during Games, I have succeeded
in avoiding rain, ice, violent exertion.

Half-time, and a plate is carried out
piled with orange slices for the players.
It's soon after the war, and oranges
are jewel-rare, the lovely colour singing
through the fog gloom of the muddy pitch.

The taste of envy – knowing myself
excluded from the world of hockey sticks
and reckless running I scorn anyway;
a milieu indifferent to A-grades,
where classmates suck the juices of the sun.

2

These seedless supermarket grapes
are acidulous clones, crisp as cucumber,
unloved makeweights for the five-a-day.
Nothing suffered to bring them to the table –
that should be consoling. But I lust
for glistening jade-green flesh, oozing juice.

I'm thinking of the vine my father planted,
clustered with plump fruit, tight purple skins
slipping off like porn stars' underwear.
And I'm remembering how she told me once
he'd drowned a neighbour's cat, and buried it
under the roots, beside the greenhouse wall.

Solitude

'Don't you get lonely?'
No, never.
This is mind's rehearsal.
I have weather
to walk in, a life's
riches laid down
like slow-formed peat.

To be alone
is to taste existence,
its small choices
brushing me like moths;
I am a dance of conscious
and unconscious moments.
That chaconne. This silence.

Shoreline

The path we all must follow,
soon or late, ends in the mind's eye

where land encounters water
and shingle shifts with the receding tide.

You approach the sea like a homecoming:
your vast origin; your (dis)solution.

You are the breather and the breathed.
The question and the questioner.

Rock with the impersonal flux,
receive from it what you can. Its message:

You are less separate than you imagine.

Float, then, at anchor for now,
rising, falling on the sea's dark breast

without effort, until the hawser,
slackening, releases you
into the oceans of the world.

Le moment juste

'I wouldn't want to drag on like that' –
as if the choice would come easily,
as if, one Tuesday, perhaps,
despite daffodils just out,
and something tasty waiting in the fridge,
we might flirt with that final *Will I? Now?*

I knew a woman who had death in the bag.
'I've saved enough pills,' she'd say.
And I've always wondered why
she tolerated that lingering end.

Maybe there were always daffodils; always
some great or tiny thing worth staying for.
Or never a moment rich enough
in meaning for a final exit –

because, if our whole life
is the story we tell ourselves,
then how can we judge
the right moment for the dénouement
when we are so close, our faces
pressed up hard against eternity?

It Turns Out

it's not the innumerable fags that will kill her,
but the asbestos factory all those hippy years ago;
and the organic vegetables no damn good at all.

Now she is waiting for results suspended between
cigarettes – though, really, suspense would be
equilibrium, a perfectly composed indifference,

not this raised heart-beat, its lurching gait
flinging her between imagined possibilities
as she stands up when they call her name.

Happening

How spacious is the happening world.
You think you might become a boy,
have seven children, all called Jonquil.

Then without noticing, step by option,
what seem like tiny routine turnings,
innocent of consequence, sweep you

into the wide mouth of the future
and you drift into a funnel
whose walls get closer, closer.

You settle for not being a boy;
even grateful at the sight of blood.
You hardly notice the sealed doors

but, look, you're in a cul-de-sac, it's dark,
and all the happening has already happened.

Less than Beautiful

All these – a wrinkled hand,
gesturing with arthritic eloquence;

a tulip splaying outwards,
just before the petals fall;

the transgressive turn-on,
double handful, of a fat, cheerful body;

robust diphthongs of the unentitled,
faces turned from sneers and silences;

Downs girl at the mirror, dreaming
with eye-liner and foundation...

So move over vapid, glamorous lookalikes.
Skinnies – make room for the stumpy.

Let's celebrate the asymmetrical,
hair that doesn't defy probability.

Out with you, cloned clothes-horses,
lying teeth, airbrushed silhouettes

because – you know what? –
you're not worth it.

April

You can hear it's spring:
rain bounces babbling along the gutters,
blossom plastered on the windscreen
squeaks the wiper blades. Birds, of course –
assertive blackbirds, winsome chaffinches –
and the soft susurration of new leaves.

Don't get snared in thoughts of transience.
The trick is to not look forward.
Don't even think about diminuendo
through July and August to when sad September
will inscribe mortality on every dusk
as radiators tick and nights close you in.

Memento Mori

(after a sequence of paintings by Helen Wilks)

Hurtling through time, as this fruit is
– starches becoming sugars,
becoming glucose, oozing rank juice –
we too are on track for dissolution.

The point is to see the beauty in it
as these paintings do – red...
blue... powdery green... blacks...
loss of definition, slow collapse.

And the trick is to resist anticipating
the time when November gales
will strip the trees of consolation, turn
our gaze earthwards to where brown

leaves inscribe mortality in every dusk;
but celebrate the reds, the blues, the blacks.

Endurance

At night this house is a fractious animal.
Oak floorboards flex and groan, shrugging the stacks
of books read and unread. Down in the hall
the cooling radiators tick and growl.

How could it not feel old, as creatures do?
It has earned the petulance that makes it
jam cupboard doors, knock pictures out of true.
It will endure long after I've passed through.

Logically

a slave can't lose his wife
since, as property himself,
there can be no 'his'.

A man can't lose his life
since, after his last breath,
he won't exist.

Only in the minds of the bereaved
is what his life could have been,
the turnings missed

and the frail legacy of one
who made marks on the world
and, one day, ceased.

Solid

You think you're solid.
Once you were hardly there
and soon again
you won't be anywhere.

Your molecules returned
to the cosmic soup.
You will be water, air,
the provisional aggregate
you struggle to preserve
dissolved to brief memories,
love, if you're lucky;
emails in the cloud
a kind of palimpsest.

For nothing goes to waste
no atom is destroyed
just redeployed.
And the molecules here now
were here when time began –
no animals, no man –
and Earth was wilderness.

But there's no denying
one day you will be dead
and where do the colours go
when the carpet fades?

CPSIA information can be obtained
at www.ICGtesting.com
Printed in the USA
JSHW022248250723
45367JS00001B/3

9 781780 376530